PIANO · VOCAL · GUITAR

DUA LIPA

ISBN 978-1-5400-2929-4

Visit Hal Leonard Online at
www.halleonard.com

Contact us:
Hal Leonard
7777 West Bluemound Road
Milwaukee, WI 53213
Email: info@halleonard.com

In Europe, contact:
Hal Leonard Europe Limited
42 Wigmore Street
Marylebone, London, W1U 2RN
Email: info@halleonardeurope.com

In Australia, contact:
Hal Leonard Australia Pty. Ltd.
4 Lentara Court
Cheltenham, Victoria, 3192 Australia
Email: info@halleonard.com.au

GENESIS

Words and Music by DUA LIPA,
CLARENCE BERNARD COFFEE, SARAH HUDSON,
ANDREAS SCHEEN SCHULLER and FERRAS ALQAISI

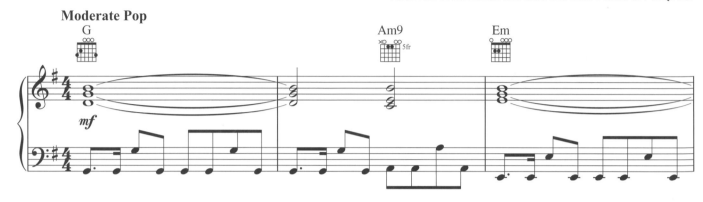

In the be - gin - ning ___ God cre - at - ed
Don't mat - ter what's writ - ten, ___ we can start all

heav - en and earth. For what it's worth, think that he might have cre - at - ed you first. ___
o - ver a - gain, all o - ver a - gain. Oh, how can I get you all o - ver my skin?

HOTTER THAN HELL

Words and Music by DUA LIPA,
TOMMY BAXTER, GERARD O'CONNELL
and ADAM MIDGLEY

Pop Dance

He calls me the de-vil, _____ I want to make him _____ sin. Ev-'ry time I _____ knock, _____ he can't help but let me in. Must be home-sick for the real, _____ I'm the real-est it

*Recorded a half step lower.

LOST IN YOUR LIGHT

Words and Music by DUA LIPA,
MICHAEL PIMENTEL and RICK NOWELS

BE THE ONE

Words and Music by JACK TARRANT,
LUCY TAYLOR and NICHOLAS GALE

wrong, I was wrong, I was wrong, come back to me, ba-by, we can

work this out.

Oh, ba-by, come on, let me get to know you, just an-oth-er chance so that I can show that I won't

let you down, oh, no, no, I won't let you down, oh, no, 'cause I could be the

BLOW YOUR MIND
(Mwah)

Words and Music by DUA LIPA,
JON LEVINE and LAUREN CHRISTY

Moderate groove

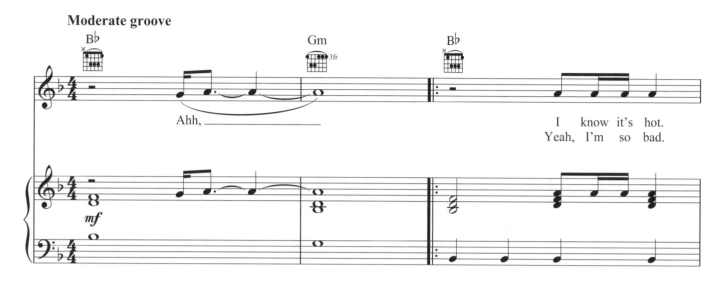

Ahh, _____

I know it's hot.
Yeah, I'm so bad.

I know we've __ got _____ some-thin' that mon-ey can't __ buy.
Best that you've __ had. __ I guess you're dig-ging the __ show.

Fight-ing to fits, bit-ing your __ lip. ___ Lov-ing too late in the __
O - pen the door, you want some __ more. ___ When you want to leave, let me __

IDGAF

Words and Music by DUA LIPA,
MNEK, SKYLER STONESTREET,
WHISKEY WATERS and LARZZ PRINCIPATO

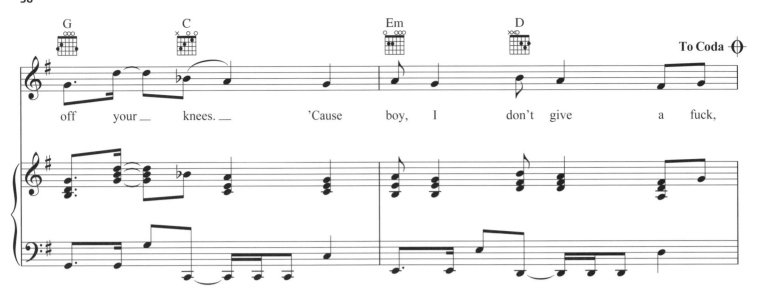

off your __ knees. __ 'Cause boy, I don't give a fuck,

ah, ah, _____ a - bout you. _____ No, I don't

give a damn. __ You keep rem - i - nis - cing on when

you were my man. ___ But I'm o - ver you. _____ Now, you're

all in the past. _____ You talk all that sweet talk, but I

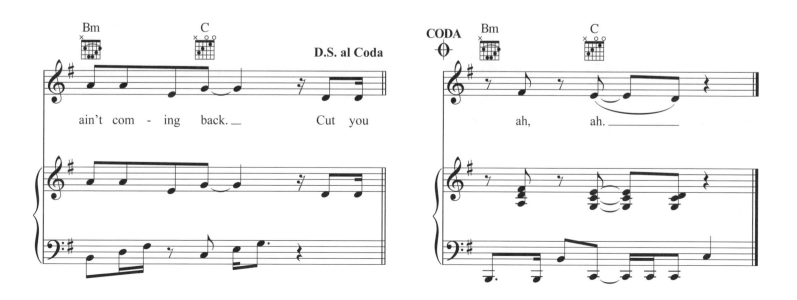

ain't com - ing back. ___ Cut you

D.S. al Coda

CODA

ah, ah. _____

GARDEN

Words and Music by DUA LIPA,
GREG WELLS and SEAN DOUGLAS

Moderately

Re-mem-ber when we swam in the o - cean? ___ Now we know what's deep in - side.

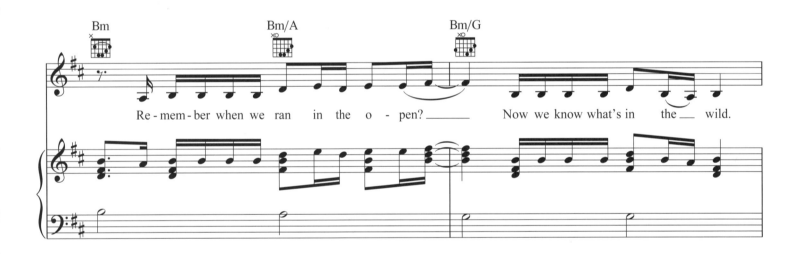

Re-mem-ber when we ran in the o - pen? ___ Now we know what's in the ___ wild.

Used to think that this love was heav - en sent. ___ How did we get lost, can't get back a - gain. ___

Recorded a half-step lower.

BEGGING

Words and Music by DUA LIPA,
CARA SALIMANDO, JAMES FLANNIGAN
and GABE SIMON

Moderate Dance groove

NO GOODBYES

Words and Music by DUA LIPA,
ISLEY JUBER, DAN TRAYNOR
and LINDY ROBBINS

Moderate Pop Ballad

THINKING 'BOUT YOU

Words and Music by DUA LIPA
and ADAM ARGYLE

Acoustic groove

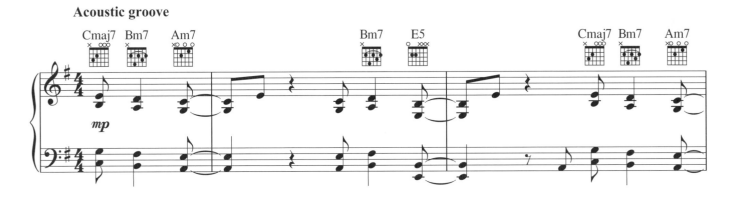

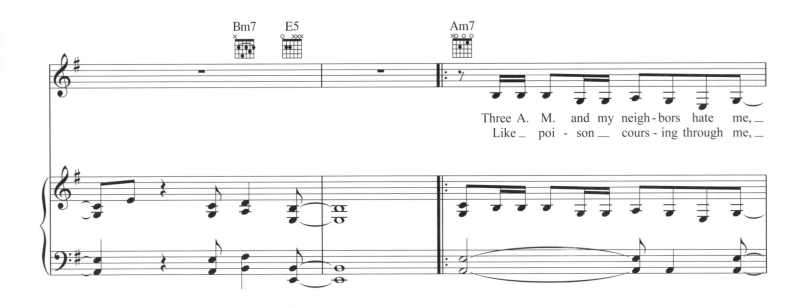

Three A. M. and my neigh-bors hate me, __
Like __ poi - son __ cours - ing through me, __

mu - sic blast - ing, shak - ing these walls. __
so __ clear my vi - sion is blurred. __

NEW RULES

Words and Music by CAROLINE AILIN,
IAN KIRKPATRICK and EMILY WARREN SCHWARTZ

To Coda

(I got new rules, I count 'em.)

(I got - ta tell them to my - self.) I keep push - ing for - wards, but he

keeps pull - ing me back - wards. (No-where to turn, no - where to turn.)

Now I'm stand-ing back from it, I fi - n'lly see the pat - tern. (I nev - er learn,

HOMESICK

Words and Music by DUA LIPA
and CHRIS MARTIN

Slow Ballad

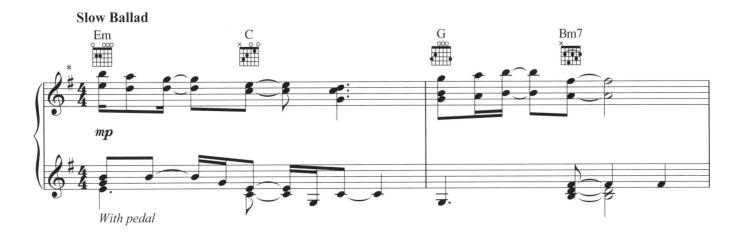

Here where the sky's fall - ing, I'm cov - ered in ____ blue. I'm

crack in my ____ win - dow, a bird in my ____ room.

* *Recorded a half step lower.*

Em C6/9 G Bm

I know, I know, I know. _ You give me a mean-ing, some-thing I can breathe in,

Em C6/9 G Bm

To Coda

I know, I know, I know. _ It's a bit-ter-sweet feel-ing, long - ing and I'm leav-ing,

Em C6/9 G/B

I go, I go, I go. ___ But I wish I was there with you. _ Oh, I

C6/9 G/B (♪ = ♪) G5 G/B C6/9 G/B

wish I was there with you. ___

5/8

You give me a rea - son, some - thing to be-lieve in, I know, I know, I know. _

You give me a mean-ing, some - thing I can breathe in, I know, I know, I know. _ It's a

bit-ter-sweet feel - ing, long - ing and I'm leav - ing, I go, I go, I go. _

DREAMS

Words and Music by DUA LIPA,
TOM NEVILLE and CHELCEE GRIMES

Syncopated Pop

Last night, my fan-ta-sies be-came oh, so true.

You said you want-ed me as much as I want you.

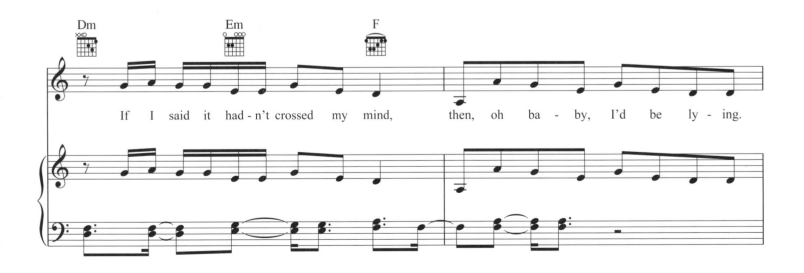

If I said it had-n't crossed my mind, then, oh ba-by, I'd be ly-ing.

It just got com - pli - cat - ed, I don't know what to do. Can I

get it like that, that, that? Let me know. 'Cause I real - ly like that, that, that when you go. And I

know it's not real, but the way that I feel, I just need to know. Can I

In my dreams. In-side, I'm scream-ing loud, I'm call-ing out your name. It's

time you start-ed lis-ten-ing, don't think you can hear me. ___

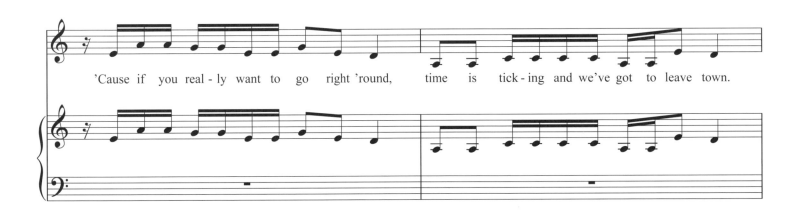

'Cause if you real-ly want to go right 'round, time is tick-ing and we've got to leave town.

D.S. al Coda

Time is tick-ing and we've got to leave town to-night. ___ Yeah, can I

ROOM 4 TWO

Words and Music by DUA LIPA,
AUTUMN ROWE and TOM NEVILLE

Steadily

Up and down, it all comes back 'round. Push and shove, do you feel bet-ter now?

Knock, knock, knock, you'll come tum-bling down. Kar-ma's got a kiss for you.
Why are you blam-

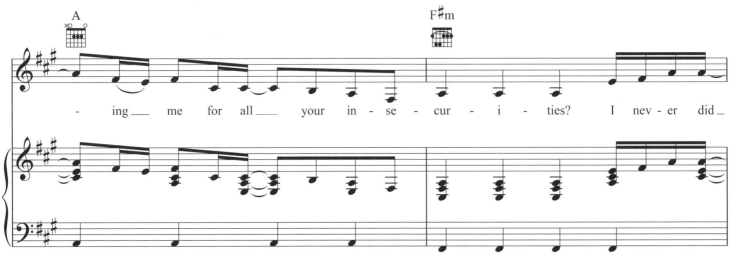

-ing __ me for all __ your in-se-cur-i -ties? I nev-er did __

NEW LOVE

Words and Music by DUA LIPA,
EMILE HAYNIE and ANDREW WYATT

Syncopated Pop beat

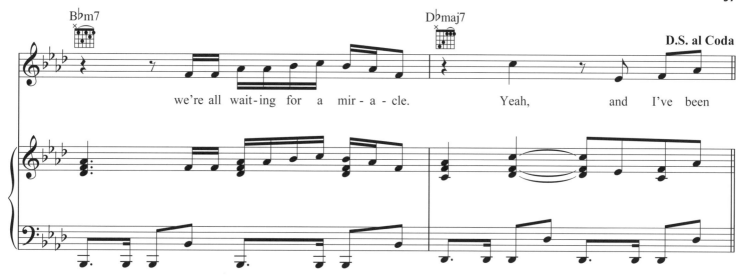

we're all wait-ing for a mir - a - cle. Yeah, and I've been

D.S. al Coda

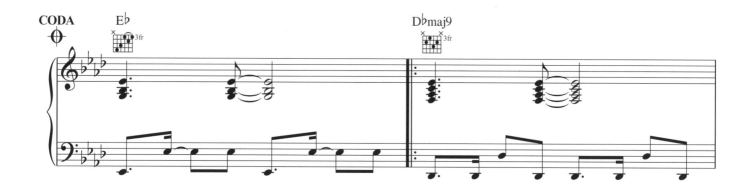

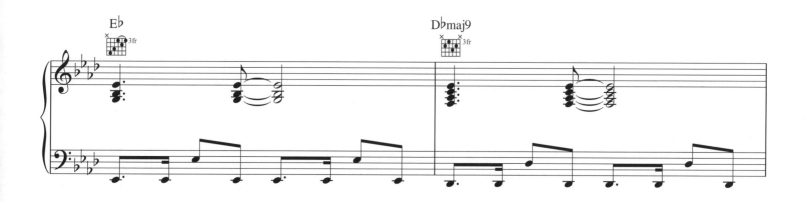

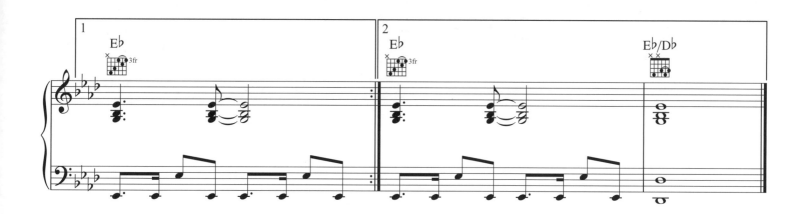

BAD TOGETHER

Words and Music by DUA LIPA,
TOM BARNES, BEN KOHN,
PETE KELLEHER and CHELCEE GRIMES

With a Pop groove

I know you're bad for me, but you know I am too.

Me and you to-geth-er, like a loved up bruise. I'll make you an of-fer that you can't re-fuse.

Ba-by, you're o-kay, ba-by, you're o-kay. No, you won't, won't go break-ing my heart. You've

* Recorded a half step lower.

I'm for you. Oh, no, I don't care what's been done here be - fore ___ me, I don't give a
(loco)

damn just as long as you care. ___ 'Cause ba - by, I've been bad, but the heav-ens for-gave ___

___ me. You don't need to ask 'cause I'm al - read - y there. ___ Let's be bad to - geth-

- er, ba - by, you and I. ___ Let's be bad to - geth-

CODA

-er. Oh, _____ yeah. ___ Let's be ___ bad, babe, ___

___ let's be ___ bad. ___ Let's be ___ bad, babe, ___ let's be ___ bad. ___

Let's be ___ bad, babe, ___ let's be ___ bad. ___ Let's be ___ bad, babe. ___

___ Oh, no, I don't care what's been done here be-fore ___ me, I don't give a

LAST DANCE

Words and Music by DUA LIPA,
STEPHEN NOEL KOZMENIUK and TALAY RILEY

Fa - tal, this at - trac - tion, yeah, we might just end up crash - ing but I'm read - y if it hap - pens with

you. ___ Meet me out in Ca - li when I'm far a - way from fam - ily and I

* Recorded a half step lower.